IMAGES
of America

THE 4,000-FOOTERS
OF NEW HAMPSHIRE'S
WHITE MOUNTAINS

D1716312

A lone hiker standing on the rim of the Great Gulf gazes toward the peaks of the Northern Presidential Range in an image from the early 1900s. (Courtesy of Appalachian Mountain Club.)

IMAGES
of America

THE 4,000-FOOTERS OF NEW HAMPSHIRE'S WHITE MOUNTAINS

Mike Dickerman

ARCADIA
PUBLISHING

Published by Arcadia Publishing
Charleston, South Carolina

Printed in the United States of America

Library of Congress Control Number: 2021931661

For all general information, please contact Arcadia Publishing:
Telephone 843-853-2070
Fax 843-853-0044
E-mail sales@arcadiapublishing.com
For customer service and orders:
Toll-Free 1-888-313-2665

Visit us on the Internet at www.arcadiapublishing.com

In memory of the late Gene Daniell, the "grand poobah" of peakbagging

CONTENTS

ACKNOWLEDGMENTS

Compiling the vintage photographs for this book has been a fun and extremely rewarding experience, but it would not have been possible without the assistance of many other individuals and organizations.

Fellow mountain enthusiasts Dave Govatski, Steve Smith, and Chris Whiton helped in varying ways and degrees. With Dave, it was having unlimited access to his incredible White Mountains postcard and photograph collection. Dave also arranged for my access to hundreds of US Forest Service images. With Steve, it was his willingness to share not just a few of his photographs but, more importantly, his incredible knowledge of the region and the 4,000-Footers in particular. With Chris, it was his generous offer to share with me the mountain photographs of his grandfather Clyde Smith, who was not only a trail builder and pack boy but also a former fire lookout and prolific sign maker.

Jeff Leich of the New England Ski Museum, based at Cannon Mountain, was helpful in securing several great images tied to the rich history of skiing the 4,000-Footers. Likewise, Peter Crane at the Mount Washington Observatory offered to track down several rare images of the Rock Pile, despite the fact that he was in the process of dismantling and moving the entire contents of the observatory's library.

Appalachian Mountain Club (AMC) archivist and historian Becky Fullerton opened up AMC's vast collection of incredible older hiking images despite a pandemic that had the club's new library at Crawford Notch in lockdown mode for much of 2020.

Others willing to share images and information included Carol Riley and the Upper Pemigewasset Historical Society of Lincoln, Preston Conklin of the Waterville Valley Historical Society, the Town of Waterville Valley, Waterville Valley Resort, the Rauner Special Collections Library at Dartmouth College, the Randolph Mountain Club, Kris Pastoriza, Karen Daniell and Debi Clark, and Larry Labonte.

I would like to also thank the good folks at Arcadia Publishing for shepherding this project along to completion, especially acquisitions editor Erin Vosgien and title manager Caroline Anderson.

Unless otherwise noted, all images are from the author's personal collection.

Key to courtesy line abbreviations:
AMC—Appalachian Mountain Club
CW—Chris Whiton
DG—Dave Govatski
MWO—Mount Washington Observatory
NESM—New England Ski Museum
RMC—Randolph Mountain Club
UPHS—Upper Pemigewasset Historical Society
WV—Town of Waterville Valley
WVR—Waterville Valley Resort
WMNF—White Mountain National Forest

INTRODUCTION

New Hampshire's iconic 4,000-Footers have been attracting outdoor enthusiasts to the White Mountains for more than two centuries. Since the days of pioneer settler Ethan Allen Crawford, who cut some of the earliest paths up 6,288-foot Mount Washington, the high peaks of the region have been the magnet that has lured visitors from near and far to this corner of New England. This remains as true today as at any time in history, as hikers and other adventurers continue to flock to the high peaks, be it by foot, car, chairlift, or train.

According to the Appalachian Mountain Club's Four Thousand Footer Committee, nearly 16,000 hikers have now climbed to the summits of the 48 official peaks on its popular peakbagging list. In recent years, in fact, the number of annual finishers has climbed to nearly 1,000 per year. This compares to the 200 or so who were finishing up the list when this author was working on the peaks back in the mid- to late 1980s. The number of hikers reaching the peaks in winter has also grown immensely over the last few decades, with more than 900 finishers as of the start of 2021.

Though they are best known today for their popularity among these same peakbaggers, the mountains have a long and fascinating history that goes far beyond the Vibram soles of modern-day trampers. And it is this history that is the focus of the many images to be found on the following pages.

The 4,000-Footers, and many other lesser peaks, have played a major role in the development of the White Mountain region from a daunting wilderness to a thriving recreational mecca. This transformation began in the mid-1800s with the development of man-made tourist attractions such as Mount Washington's first carriage road, the world-famous Cog Railway, and the addition of various summit hotels atop the Northeast's highest peak. This was followed with the cutting of hundreds of miles of recreational footpaths in the mountain valleys and on their steep slopes and, later, the creation of some of New England's first downhill ski runs on Mounts Moosilauke, Cannon, Tecumseh, and Wildcat in the 1920s and 1930s.

While Mount Washington and the Presidential Range possess a lion's share of this history, other regions within the Whites have a long and fascinating history of their own. Take Franconia Notch, for instance, where early footpaths led hikers to the heights of Mount Lafayette and stunning Franconia Ridge, while valley-bound tourists gazed in wonderment at the famous Old Man of the Mountain rock profile on Cannon Mountain's easternmost spur peak. A bit farther south, in the remote Waterville Valley region, visitors to this secluded spot that is surrounded by a ring of 4,000-foot peaks helped establish what is generally considered the first true network of hiking trails in the country, several of which reached up to the highest peaks towering above the valley.

Intensive lumbering activity throughout the White Mountains between 1875 and 1920 also played a key role in the further development of the region as a major tourist attraction, and more than a few of the 4,000-foot mountains were heavily impacted by the logging undertaken by folks like James E. Henry, the Lincoln-based timber baron who let loose a small army of lumberjacks that invaded the vast wilderness area drained by the East Branch of the Pemigewasset River. This logging activity, and its detrimental impact on the immediate region (and the rivers flowing south out of the mountains), led to successful efforts to permanently preserve and protect the region for future generations with the establishment of several state forest reservations in the mountains and the eventual formation of the federal White Mountain National Forest.

As the 4,000-Footers are today closely tied to the hiking community, the following pages necessarily include many images tied to a century-long effort to build a coherent, connected network of footpaths and backcountry shelters in all corners of the White Mountains. The Boston-based Appalachian Mountain Club, formed in 1876, devoted much of its early activities to exploring and cutting new trails in the White Mountains. AMC's work was especially prominent along the Northern Presidential Range and the interior Pemigewasset Wilderness region. Likewise, other, smaller trail clubs, such as the Wonalancet Out Door Club in the southern Whites and the Randolph Mountain Club far to the north, were formed to develop their own local trail systems.

In the course of preparing this book, I also decided to touch briefly upon some of the individuals who either had close links to the 4,000-Footers or are among the mountains' most celebrated visitors. Over the years, the 4,000-Footers have attracted people from all walks of life. The list includes US presidents Ulysses S. Grant and Rutherford B. Hayes, both of whom visited Mount Washington while holding office. It also includes renowned 20th-century poet Robert Frost, a frequent visitor to Franconia Notch and Mount Lafayette; world-class skiers Jean-Claude Killy (of France) and Bode Miller (Easton, New Hampshire); and longtime US Supreme Court associate justice William O. Douglas.

With such a rich and fascinating history, the accompanying photographs compiled in this volume barely scratch the surface of the history surrounding New Hampshire's highest mountains. It is my hope that, at the very least, these images provide readers with a better overall understanding and appreciation of the mountains and trails that so many of us have fallen in love with over the years.

Listed below are White Mountain 4,000-Footers by elevation rank. (The first number shows traditional US Geological Survey summit elevations; the second figure reflects new Lidar elevations.)

1. Washington 6,288 feet (6,287)
2. Adams 5,799 feet (5,797)
3. Jefferson 5,716 feet (5,714)
4. Monroe 5,372 feet (5,371)
5. Madison 5,366 feet (5,363)
6. Lafayette 5,260 feet (5,243)
7. Lincoln 5,089 feet (5,080)
8. South Twin 4,902 feet (4,899)
9. Carter Dome 4,832 feet (4,840)
10. Moosilauke 4,802 feet (4,800)
11. North Twin 4,761 feet (4,759)
12. Eisenhower 4,760 feet (4,763)
13. Carrigain 4,700 feet (4,680)
14. Bond 4,698 feet (4,696)
15. Middle Carter 4,610 feet (4,624)
16. West Bond 4,540 feet (4,518)
17. Garfield 4,500 feet (4,501)
18. Liberty 4,459 feet (4,457)
19. South Carter 4,430 feet (4,445)
20. Wildcat 4,422 feet (4,399)
21. North Hancock 4,420 feet (4,398)
22. South Kinsman 4,358 feet (4,356)
23. (T) Field 4,340 feet (4,326)
23. (T) Osceola 4,340 feet (4,329)

25. Flume 4,328 feet (4,329)
26. South Hancock 4,319 feet (4,257)
27. Pierce 4,310 feet (4,315)
28. North Kinsman 4,293 feet (4,274)
29. Willey 4,285 feet (4,299)
30. Bondcliff 4,265 feet (4,263)
31. Zealand 4,260 feet (4,264)
32. North Tripyramid 4,180 feet (4,160)
33. Cabot 4,170 feet (4,161)
34. East Osceola 4,156 feet (4,161)
35. Middle Tripyramid 4,140 feet (4,135)
36. Cannon 4,100 feet (4,083)
37. Wildcat D 4,062 feet (4,060)
38. Hale 4,054 feet (4,067)
39. Jackson 4,052 feet (4,052)
40. Tom 4,051 feet (4,048)
41. Moriah 4,049 feet (4,047)
42. Passaconaway 4,043 feet (4,079)
43. Owl's Head 4,025 feet (4,029)
44. Galehead 4,024 feet (4,029)
45. Whiteface 4,020 feet (4,018)
46. Waumbek 4,006 feet (4,011)
47. (T) Isolation 4,003 feet (4,004)
47. (T) Tecumseh 4,003 feet (3,995)

One

Mount Washington and the Presidential Range

Late-19th-century visitors to Mount Washington, the highest peak in the northeastern United States, assemble in front of the original Tip-Top House, one of the earliest summit hotels atop the 6,288-foot peak.

For nearly 170 years, Mount Washington's summit has been the site of various man-made structures, including seasonal hotels, weather observatories, and visitor centers. Visible in this aerial view from 1965 are the second Summit House hotel, the Mount Washington Auto Road, and the oldest surviving mountaintop structure, the Tip-Top House. Rearing up behind Mount Washington and across the Great Gulf are the rugged, undeveloped peaks of the Northern Presidential Range. (Courtesy of WMNF.)

Situated approximately one and a half miles southwest of Mount Washington's summit is the Appalachian Mountain Club's popular Lakes of the Clouds Hut, which has been entertaining seasonal guests since 1915. At an elevation of 5,012 feet and just above treeline in the alpine zone, the hut and its two namesake lakes are only accessible by trail, and hikers must not only navigate steep terrain but also contend with potentially deadly weather.

Mount Washington remains the lone 4,000-Footer that is accessible to visitors by road. The Mount Washington Auto Road (originally known as the Mount Washington Carriage Road) runs about eight and a half miles from the former Glen House site on the Pinkham Notch Highway (Route 16) to the summit via a series of sweeping switchbacks. Construction of the road was begun in 1855 under the direction of engineer Charles H. Cavis, and after several fits and starts, work was completed six years later, with the toll road officially opening for public use on August 8, 1861. For the first four decades of the road's existence, summit visitors took horse-drawn carriages and coaches to the mountaintop, where they could enjoy the scenery and, if they chose, stay overnight at one of the summit hotels. With the invention of the automobile, however, cars became the preferred mode of transportation over the road, and horse travel gradually disappeared.

No. 1243.   View from Mt. Washington Summit House.

Just a few years after the Carriage Road opened on the eastern slopes of Mount Washington, an ambitious project to bring rail service to the summit on its western slopes was started in the summer of 1866. The Cog Railway was the brainchild of Campton, New Hampshire, native Sylvester Marsh, and though the idea of building a railroad up the mountain was ridiculed at first, Marsh was able to obtain a patent for his unique mountain-climbing train and form the Mount Washington Steam Railway Company. After three years of construction, trains started running to the summit by July 4, 1869, with fares of $3 (one way) and $4 (round-trip). In the above stereoscopic image, one of the Cog's earliest engines is pictured at the summit, while below, the engine *Cloud* is seen as it prepares for a ride up the mountain in the early 1870s.

Along its three-mile-long route, the Cog Railway line climbs more than 3,700 feet from the base station to the summit, with the steepest stretch running along Jacob's Ladder, the long, high trestle with a maximum grade of 37.41 percent. The roadbed of the Cog closely follows the original route of a footpath to the summit blazed in the early 1820s by local pioneer settler Ethan Allen Crawford.

The Cog Railway's original engine, named *Hero*, and more famously known as *Peppersass*, operated for a dozen years before being "retired" from service in 1878. After serving as a traveling exhibit for many years, it was returned to the mountain, put back into working order, and enlisted to make a triumphant run up the mountain on July 20, 1929. Tragically, a mechanical failure during its descent caused the engine to career wildly down the tracks, resulting in a crash that killed photographer Daniel Rossiter.

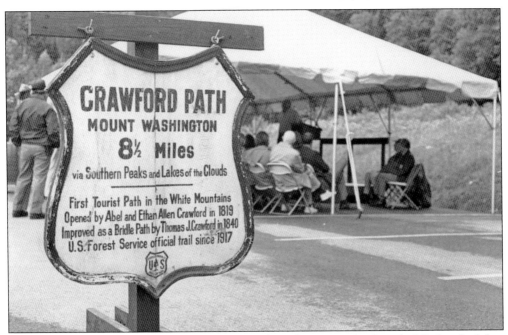

Perhaps the most famous footpath along the Presidential Range is the Crawford Path, which has long been considered the oldest continuously maintained hiking trail in the nation. Constructed in 1819 by Ethan Allen Crawford, the trail runs eight and a half miles from Crawford Notch to the summit of Mount Washington and crosses over or near all the major peaks of the southern Presidentials. This photograph was taken in 1994 at an event marking the 175th anniversary of its opening.

Another historical trail along the southern Presidentials is the century-old Edmands Path up Mount Eisenhower. Reconstructed in 1909 by pioneer trail builder John Rayner Edmands, the path closely follows the route of an old bridle path and in its upper reaches is well regarded for its unusually comfortable grade amidst such difficult terrain. In the accompanying image, one can see the almost sidewalk-like nature of the trail. (Courtesy of DG.)

With its broad, bald dome and massive presence along the southern Presidential Range, it seems only appropriate that 4,760-foot Mount Eisenhower bears the name of one of America's greatest mid-20th-century figures. For a century and a half, the peak was known simply as Mount Pleasant, but an act of the New Hampshire legislature in 1969 led to the official renaming of the peak three years later in honor of World War II general and former US president Dwight D. Eisenhower. At a 1972 event marking the name change, the Eisenhower family was well represented, as in attendance was Julie Nixon Eisenhower, the daughter of then-president Richard Nixon and the wife of David Eisenhower, Ike's grandson.

While many forested areas of the White Mountains succumbed to the axes of late-19th- and early-20th-century loggers, pockets of virgin timber survived the massive cuttings that were so commonplace 100 years ago. In this undated image taken on the lower slopes of Mount Jackson in the southern Presidentials, an unidentified man poses amidst an extensive stand of old-growth spruce averaging 90 feet in height with a diameter of 15 to 26 inches. (Courtesy of WMNF.)

On April 13, 1913, the New Hampshire state legislature honored the nation's 14th president, Franklin Pierce, by renaming one of the Presidential Range peaks after the Granite State native. Mount Pierce (4,310 feet) was originally known as Mount Clinton, in honor of former New York governor and senator DeWitt Clinton. The peak was also referred to as "Bald Hill" by pioneer settler Ethan Allen Crawford.

From the summit of Mount Pierce to all points north along the Presidential Range, hikers find themselves trekking mostly above treeline, with expansive views in all directions (at least on cloudless days). Here, a party of trampers in the mid-1960s is seen approaching the sharp summit crest of 5,732-foot Mount Monroe, the fourth-highest peak in the White Mountains. (Courtesy of AMC.)

Lakes of the Clouds Hut, located on a shelf at the base of Mount Monroe, is today the largest of AMC's eight mountain huts and can accommodate as many as 90 overnight guests during its summer-only season of operation. This postcard view shows how the original hut looked in 1922, the year it underwent the first of three subsequent renovations and expansions.

The three major peaks of the Northern Presidential Range are well known for their rugged nature, which is characterized often by jumbles of loose rock and innumerable jagged outcrops. A prime example is Castellated Ridge, which extends northwest from the summit of Mount Jefferson (5,716 feet). The AMC *White Mountain Guide* calls this "the sharpest and most salient of the White Mountain Ridges." (Courtesy of DG.)

With a summit elevation of 5,799 feet, sharp-crested Mount Adams is the second-highest peak in the White Mountains, dwarfed only by its close neighbor to the south, Mount Washington. Like most of the Presidential Range summits, it was named in July 1820 when Ethan Allen Crawford guided a party of hikers to the top of Mount Washington, and its members proceeded to bestow monikers on all the high peaks. In this case, the mountain was named for the nation's second president, John Adams (1735–1826). (Courtesy of AMC.)

Some of the wildest terrain along the Northern Presidentials is found on the northern slope of Mount Adams in King Ravine. The 1,100-foot headwall was first climbed in 1857 by Rev. Thomas Starr King and local guide James Gordon in an epic nine-hour adventure. In this classic postcard view taken by local photographer Guy Shorey, an ambitious climber poses atop a sharp outcrop at the so-called "Gateway" to King Ravine. (Courtesy of DG.)

Hikers negotiating the boulder-strewn, 1,100-foot headwall of King Ravine face a daunting task with many obstacles to contend with. The ravine is named for Rev. Thomas Starr King, author of the classic book *The White Hills*, published in 1859. Starr King called the ravine "the most spacious and grandest of all the gorges that have been cloven out of the White Hills." (Courtesy of DG.)

Dramatic stretches of open, rocky terrain are not unusual throughout the northern peaks of the Presidentials. Although the exact location of this spectacular ridge is not identified by the photographer, it is likely that it is somewhere along the northern peaks, with Caps Ridge on Mount Jefferson a strong possibility. (Courtesy of DG.)

In 1956, the US Forest Service erected this Quonset-style emergency shelter in the col between Mounts Jefferson and Adams, considered one of the most potentially hazardous locations in the mountains. The Edmands Col shelter was supposed to be used only for refuge from poor weather, but increased use by backpackers and resulting damage to the fragile alpine vegetation in the vicinity resulted in the removal of the structure by 1982. (Courtesy of AMC.)

The Appalachian Mountain Club's famed string of backcountry huts got its start in 1888 when the club constructed Madison Spring Hut in the Adams-Madison Col. Opened the following year, the stone structure cost just over $700 to build. The original hut fell victim to a devastating fire in October 1940, but under the direction of huts manager Joe Dodge, a replacement hut (seen here) was rebuilt and open for service by August 1941.

As the Cog Railway line nears the summit cone of Mount Washington, trains pass close by the lip of the Great Gulf, another of the deep glacial cirques that dominate the landscape of the Presidential Range. Seen here rising above and behind the Cog train is Mount Jefferson, which lies to the west of the Great Gulf.

2314. Gulf of Mexico, Mt. Washington.

As noted on the above stereoscopic view from the late 1800s, the Great Gulf was, for reasons unknown, sometimes referred to as the "Gulf of Mexico." Ethan Allen Crawford, while leading a group of mountain explorers in 1829, supposedly came up with the more recognizable name for the glacial basin when he and his companions emerged out of the clouds and wandered over to the edge of "a great gulf."

Remote Spaulding Lake (above), situated deep in the heart of the Great Gulf, has long been a popular destination for ambitious hikers, and rightly so. As author Steven D. Smith writes in his guidebook, *Ponds and Lakes of the White Mountains*, "Its setting might be the most spectacular of any White Mountain pond." At an elevation of 4,228 feet, the tiny mountain tarn is one of the highest bodies of water in the region, and its setting in the shadow of the Great Gulf's headwall is impressive. The lake was explored early on by botanist James Robbins, who first visited in 1829. Tip-Top House manager John H. Spaulding paid the lake a visit in 1853 and gave it his family name. The first trail to Spaulding Lake and the Great Gulf headwall was established in 1881 by local guide Benjamin Osgood, while AMC built a small shelter (below) along an improved Great Gulf Trail in 1909. (Below, courtesy of DG.)

Fashionably dressed members of the Appalachian Mountain Club celebrated Independence Day in style back in 1893 with a July 4 visit to the Perch, a birchbark shelter high up on Mount Adams that had been constructed the previous summer by J. Rayner Edmands and two local guides. This visit coincided with the club's annual field meeting being held in nearby Jefferson. (Courtesy of AMC.)

Male and female visitors to Mount Washington are shown here posing for a photograph on their way to Tuckerman Ravine by way of the Raymond Path. This path, first blazed in 1863 by Maj. Curtis B. Raymond and still in existence today, links the Auto Road to Tuckerman Ravine. This party of trampers was apparently headed into the ravine to view Tuckerman's well-known early summer attraction, the Snow Arch. (Courtesy of DG.)

Getting to the eastern base of Presidential Range peaks was no easy chore in the pre-automobile days. This undated image shows the rough-and-tumble Pinkham Notch Road, with Mount Washington and distinct Tuckerman Ravine (upper left corner) clearly visible high above.

This Guy Shorey postcard was taken at the site of the former Glen House and the base of the Mount Washington Auto Road, which can just be seen in the lower right corner where it enters the forested lower slopes of the mountain. (Courtesy of DG.)

Before recurring landslides and wind-thrown trees forced the closure of the former Cascade Ravine Trail, this waterfall on the lower slopes of Mount Adams was frequented by many Randolph-based mountain climbers. Cascade Ravine, a non-glacial ravine, lies between Nowell and Israel Ridges and is drained by Cascade Brook.

Two

FRANCONIA NOTCH AND THE WESTERN WHITE MOUNTAINS

Snow-capped Franconia Ridge, with Mount Lafayette (5,260 feet) seen just left of center and Mount Lincoln (5,089 feet) on the right, is one of the featured attractions of much-visited Franconia Notch in the western White Mountains. The ridge, photographed here from the summit of neighboring Cannon Mountain, is the highest in the region outside of the Presidential Range. (Courtesy of CW.)

It is not just hikers who have long enjoyed visiting the heights of Franconia Notch. Since 1938, the Cannon Mountain Aerial Tramway has whisked visitors from the floor of the Notch to the summit of state-owned Cannon Mountain (4,100 feet). The tramway, the first of its kind in North America, officially opened on June 28, 1938, with hundreds of invited guests and others in attendance. In its first summer of operation, more than 100,000 passengers were ferried more than 2,000 vertical feet from the base station to the summit station, and an additional 37,000 riders utilized the tram during the ensuing ski season. In the image at left, taken on the tramway's opening day, a tram car approaches the summit station, and below, spectators watch as the tram car reaches its summit destination. (Both, courtesy of AMC.)

Cannon Mountain has long been associated with the famous Old Man of the Mountain natural rock formation, which collapsed into a heap of rubble in May 2003. The rock profile was supposedly first spotted in 1805 by local men Luke Brooks and Francis Whitcomb while working with a survey crew in Franconia Notch along the shores of what would become known as Profile Lake. Over time, the Old Man, with its stern visage, came to symbolize Granite Staters' self-professed individualism and independence and was incorporated into many aspects of New Hampshire life. To this day, the Old Man's likeness continues to adorn state license plates and highway signs. Despite decades of effort to save the Old Man from falling from its cliff-top perch, it ultimately fell victim to the naturally occurring freeze/thaw cycle and met its sad demise in the overnight hours of May 2 and 3, 2003.

Undoubtedly one of the most photographed natural features in the White Mountains, the Old Man of the Mountain is depicted here in a stereoscopic view published in 1880 by Kilburn Brothers of Littleton, New Hampshire.

Cannon Mountain's name is derived from this oblong rock formation near the summit that, when viewed from below, resembles a cannon. Over the past two centuries, the mountain has also been identified on various published maps as Freak Mountain (per Philip Carrigain's 1816 map of the state), Profile Mountain, Old Man's Mountain, and Mount Jackson (presumably for the nation's seventh president, Andrew Jackson).

One of the region's most famous grand hotels, the Profile House, sat at the base of Cannon Mountain in Franconia Notch and was a convenient base for ambitious guests to explore the local mountain scenery. Just steps away were early hiking trails up Cannon and Mount Lafayette. Also a short distance away was the lakeside vista of the famous Old Man of the Mountain. The first Profile House, pictured above, was razed in October 1905 to make way for a more modern structure to be known as the New Profile House. Bolstered by a construction crew of 300 men, the new hotel (below) was built during the ensuing winter months and entertained its first guests by July 1906. Unfortunately, the New Profile House stood for less than two decades, as it was destroyed by fire in August 1923.

Hikers and other visitors to Cannon Mountain's summit viewing platform enjoy a bird's-eye view of the western White Mountains in this Roland Peabody image taken in 1941. Peabody was the longtime manager at Cannon and an instrumental figure in transforming the mountain into a major ski destination.

During the winter season, skiers have been taking on Cannon's challenging slopes for nearly 90 years. The state-run ski area was aided greatly in its early years by the addition of the Aerial Tramway. Here, a downhill Cannon skier soaks in the stunning scenery during a February 1954 visit to the Franconia, New Hampshire, landmark. Among the mountain's most famous homegrown skiers is Olympic medalist Bode Miller.

The first trail in New England cut specifically for downhill ski racing was the Richard Taft Trail, which began at Cannon Mountain's summit and extended westward up and over a sub-peak called Mount Jackson. The idea of cutting the race trail was pushed by Kate Peckett of nearby Sugar Hill, who operated the first resort-based ski school in the nation at Peckett's–on–Sugar Hill. It was a two-year project to cut the trail, with the newly formed Civilian Conservation Corps (CCC) providing much of the manpower in the second year. In the ensuing years, the Taft hosted many major ski races, including the 1946 US Nationals, the first national championship to be held since the start of World War II. The image to the right is from March 1938, and the image below depicts hikers on Bald Mountain enjoying a bird's-eye view of the race trail. (Right, courtesy of AMC; below, courtesy of DG.)

With a summit elevation of 5,260 feet, Mount Lafayette is the sixth-highest peak in the White Mountains and the highest outside of the Presidential Range. Lafayette sits across Franconia Notch from Cannon Mountain, and its upper reaches lie above treeline and within the alpine vegetation zone. This image shows Lafayette as seen from Cannon, with the Appalachian Mountain Club's Greenleaf Hut visible on a shoulder of the main peak.

Mount Lafayette sits at the north end of the scenic Franconia Range, with the sister 4,000-Footer peaks of Mounts Lincoln, Liberty, and Flume just to the south. Here, a hiker atop Lafayette scans the horizon to the west as the narrow ridgeline continues on toward Mount Lincoln, just under a mile away. The hike along the popular Franconia Ridge Trail is considered one of the most scenic footpaths in New England.

Though it has been a few years now since any such major event, rock landslides have been an ever-present threat in Franconia Notch for at least 200 years, with multiple slides occurring during the time span, most on the lower slopes of Mount Lafayette and its neighboring Franconia Ridge peaks. The major landslide from 1959 shown here was one of several in the last century to cross and block the state highway through the Notch. In this instance, 200 feet of the highway was buried under 27 feet of landslide debris, requiring nearly four days of around-the-clock work to get the road open again to motor vehicle traffic. Fortunately, none of the Franconia Notch landslides have resulted in fatalities.

For a time in the mid-1800s, the summit of Mount Lafayette was home to a crude stone hut that accommodated overnight guests during the warmer months of the year. The Mount Lafayette Summit House, pictured here, was only in operation for a decade or so, though the exact date of its closure is not known. Sections of the building's stone foundation are still visible at the summit today.

The Appalachian Mountain Club's Greenleaf Hut is where modern-day hikers go for overnight visits on Mount Lafayette. Greenleaf was opened in 1930, with much of the funding coming by way of a bequest from former Profile House owner Col. Charles Greenleaf. The hut is situated on a western spur of Lafayette near a small body of water named Eagle Lake.

Towards the southern end of the Franconia Range is 4,459-foot Mount Liberty, located 3.8 miles south of Mount Lafayette and 4 miles distant by the shortest trail route. Seen here towering high above the Indian Head Resort along Route 3 in Lincoln, Liberty is wooded almost to its summit, where a distinct rock outcropping provides a 360-degree view of the surrounding mountain landscape.

Since the early 1900s, a campsite high up on Mount Liberty's slopes has been welcoming overnight backpackers of all ages. Liberty Spring Campsite originally housed a small open shelter accommodating six hikers. New, bigger shelters were built in 1922 and 1939 but have since been replaced by tent platforms. Here's how the campsite, with a view north towards Cannon Mountain, appeared in 1953. (Courtesy of CW.)

Mount Liberty's sharp, rocky summit is one of distinction among the White Mountain 4,000-Footers. It has one of the best, if not the best, views into the nearby Pemigewasset Wilderness Area. It also provides a unique angle north (above) towards the higher summits of Franconia Ridge and south (below) towards slide-scarred Mount Flume, its nearest neighbor just one trail mile away. It is not known how or when Mount Liberty received its name, but an 1852 *Harper's Magazine* article describing the scenic mountains of the Franconia Notch region does make mention of the peak by its given name. (Both, courtesy of AMC.)

Mt. Flume from Mt. Liberty

While Mounts Flume and Liberty get more than their share of visitors in the course of the year, a natural landmark at the base of both peaks attracts tens of thousands of guests each summer and fall. The 700-foot-long Flume Gorge is a narrow rock canyon between 10 and 20 feet wide through which Avalanche Brook flows. The flume was first discovered in 1808 by 93-year-old "Aunt Jess" Guernsey, who stumbled across it while on a fishing trip. It has been a major White Mountain attraction ever since, with several grand hotels once in operation within a short walk of its entrance at the south end of Franconia Notch. Prior to 1883, a large egg-shaped boulder (seen above) hung suspended between the flume's rock walls, but a massive landslide on June 20, 1883, permanently swept the boulder from its tight perch.

The main summit mass of Mount Flume (4,328 feet) was also permanently scarred by the same landslide activity of June 1883 that took out the Flume boulder mentioned previously. Nearly 140 years after the fact, several summit-to-base slides still scar the steep west-facing slope of Mount Flume. As noted in one hiking guidebook: "When viewed from Mount Liberty's summit, Flume's impressive slides angle down and away from the summit at a grade seemingly impossible to negotiate." For visitors to Flume's narrow summit ridge, which is no more than 8–10 feet wide, the view looking down the slides from above is dizzying. In this image, taken sometime after a 1908 forest fire consumed more than 400 acres of land on Mounts Liberty and Flume, the mountain's slide-scarred slopes are evident. (Courtesy of AMC.)

Intensive logging in the late 19th and early 20th centuries created much havoc on the lower slopes of the Franconia Range. On both the eastern and western flanks of the range, the ongoing lumbering activity forced the closure or rerouting of several existing hiking paths. Unseemly clear-cutting like that shown here on Mount Liberty's slopes ignited grassroots efforts to help save northern New Hampshire's remaining forestland. (Courtesy of WMNF.)

Timber cut on the east side of the Franconia Range was hauled out of the woods by rail on J.E. Henry's East Branch & Lincoln Railroad (EB&L). While most of the EB&L operated on standard-gauge rails, a short narrow-gauge line operated on the lower slopes of Osseo Peak in Lincoln. Modern-day hikers ascending Mount Flume via the Osseo Trail pass over a short section of this old rail bed.

On the extended ridge south of Cannon Mountain are two additional 4,000-Footers, though neither summit has the rich history of the other Franconia Notch peaks. North and South Kinsman lie less than a mile apart and are both traversed by the Georgia-to-Maine Appalachian Trail (AT). As northbound AT hikers will attest, the ascent of South Kinsman (4,358 feet) from Harrington Pond (pictured here) is one of the most grueling stretches of the AT in the Whites. (Courtesy of AMC.)

MT. KINSMAN FROM SPOONER HOUSE, 42K. FRANCONIA, N.H.

This undated postcard from the Spooner Farm in Franconia shows the layout of Kinsman Ridge as seen from the west. The tall peak visible on the right is North Kinsman (4,293 feet), while immediately to the left are the rounded summits of the three Cannon Balls, and on the far left is a section of Cannon Mountain.

North Kinsman, viewed here from the Appalachian Trail near Kinsman Pond, holds the dubious distinction of being the only peak on the White Mountain 4,000-Footer List that has never been the final summit for any finisher. Virtually all hikers "bag" the two Kinsmans in a single trip that takes them first to the top of North Kinsman and then on to the summit of South Kinsman. (Courtesy of CW.)

The Kinsmans have their own miniature version of Flume Gorge, though it is much less of an attraction. Kinsman Flume was first discovered in 1880 and was known locally for many years as Howland's Flume. Write-ups in several local newspapers, including the tourist-based *White Mountain Echo and Tourists' Register* of Bethlehem, brought it instant fame. In the accompanying image, taken at the lower end of the narrow gorge, a bridge or boardwalk spanning the flume can be seen. Though the bridge over the gorge is long gone, hikers can still access the flume via the Mount Kinsman Trail off New Hampshire Route 116 in the Easton Valley on the west side of the Kinsman Range. A short side path 2.1 miles from the start of the trail leads 150 yards to the upper end of Kinsman Flume. (Courtesy of Kris Pastoriza.)

One of the most spectacular roadside vistas in the Franconia Notch region is the view up to the Cannon Cliffs from Route 3/Interstate 93. With a height of 1,000 feet, this makes it the biggest rock face in the East, and the cliffs have long been renowned for their many rock and ice climbing routes. For perspective, the former Old Man of the Mountain rock profile was situated at the north end of the cliffs.

Nineteenth-century writer and fishing enthusiast William C. Prime built this small cabin on the eastern shore of Lonesome Lake, another Franconia Notch–area gem. The 14-acre lake, situated on a plateau just south of Cannon Mountain at an elevation of 2,740 feet, was discovered by Prime during a fishing expedition in 1859. Years later, the cabin was incorporated into the Appalachian Mountain Club's newly opened Lonesome Lake Hut facility.

Three

THE HEART OF
THE MOUNTAINS

Garfield Pond Shelter, a popular wilderness camping destination between 1920 and 1970, is depicted here in an image from 1938. The first shelter at Garfield Pond, a small (one and a half acres) tarn situated on the high shoulder of Mount Garfield, was built in 1916 after completion of the Garfield Ridge Trail connecting Mount Lafayette with Mount Garfield. It was reconstructed by the US Forest Service in 1925.

Mount Carrigain was one of several White Mountain 4,000-Footers to host a summit fire lookout in the first half of the 20th century. The New Hampshire Timberland Owners Association constructed the first mountaintop tower in 1910, with the US Forest Service operating the lookout from 1934 to 1948. In this image from the early 1920s, forest crews are pictured taking a break next to an older tower (left) and what appears to be a newly constructed observation tower. (Courtesy of WMNF.)

The deforestation of the central White Mountains during the late 19th and early 20th centuries scarred the slopes of many of the major peaks. In this image taken on Mount Carrigain, federal and state officials, including Henry S. Graves (far left), chief forester of the US Forest Service, and WMNF supervisor J.J. Fritz (second from left), view firsthand the slash left behind by years of logging activity. (Courtesy of WMNF.)

The Mount Carrigain fire lookout's cabin was located about a half-mile below the 4,700-foot summit and a short distance above the mountain's Signal Ridge, an open ridgecrest with stunning views of the region. In this image from 1934, an unidentified hiker knocks on the door of the small log structure. (Courtesy of AMC.)

This wooden observation tower adorned Carrigain's summit in the summer of 1934, when members of the Appalachian Mountain Club paid a visit to the mountaintop. Note that three of the hikers have their cameras ready in hand, while the two sitting at the top appear to be enjoying a well-earned lunch. (Courtesy of AMC.)

In the winter of 1927, this group of outdoor enthusiasts from the Appalachian Mountain Club took the East Branch & Lincoln Railroad into the nearby wilderness and got a rare opportunity to explore along the cutover slopes of seldom-visited Mount Hancock, deep in the heart of the vast central White Mountains region. Note the logging tote roads in the background. (Courtesy of UPHS.)

Two of the most remote 4,000-Footers, North and South Hancock, are named in honor of John Hancock, the first patriot to sign the Declaration of Independence. Prior to 1871, when state geologist Charles Hitchcock bestowed the name on this large mountain mass, it was identified on early maps as Pemigewasset Peak, owing to its proximity to the East Branch of the Pemigewasset River.

In the years before a maintained hiking trail was cut up the mountain's slopes, the most popular route up North Hancock was via the steep, south-facing Arrow Slide, seen here on the right from the upper reaches of South Hancock. Today's Hancock Loop Trail up North Hancock stays well to the right (or east) of the slide. (Courtesy of AMC.)

The completion in 1959 of the Conway-to-Lincoln Kancamagus Highway and the creation of the AMC Four Thousand Footer Club in 1957 sparked a sudden surge of interest in hiking to the Hancocks. Prior to the opening of the Kanc, which passes within five miles of the summits, a multi-day backpacking trip was required to bag the two peaks. This image shows the well-known hairpin curve along the Kanc near the main trailhead to the Hancocks. (Courtesy of WMNF.)

Logging railroad grades along the East Branch of the Pemigewasset River and its various branches have long served as major trunk routes to many of the region's higher summits. As evidenced by its many trail signs, North Fork Junction along the East Branch was one of the more important locales of the interior Pemi Wilderness. (Courtesy of AMC.)

The ragged cliff face atop Bondcliff (4,625 feet) has long been one of the most photogenic spots among the 4,000-Footers. The cliff face drops off several hundred feet into the valley of Hellgate Brook to the southwest, while the slide-scarred cliffs of nearby West Bond provide a most dramatic background. Bondcliff was one of the last peaks officially added to the 4,000-Footer list, gaining entry around 1980.

The high peaks of the Bond Range are seen above and beyond this operating lumber camp along the Cedar Brook valley near Mount Hancock. Camp 24, the largest of the Parker-Young Company's rail-side timber camps, is pictured here in the 1930s, when logging crews were harvesting what was left of merchantable timber in the East Branch valley. (Courtesy of UPHS.)

Since 1913, when AMC constructed a new overnight shelter near a spring between Mounts Guyot and Bond, Guyot Shelter has proven to be one of the most popular backpacking destinations among hikers venturing into the high country of the Pemi. The log structure shown here in 1938 was replaced by a new shelter the following year.

Though the wooded summit of Mount Zealand (4,260 feet) provides no views, the view from the Zeacliffs, an eastern spur of the mountain, features one of the most dramatic vistas in the central White Mountains. The main attraction in this 1934 image is slide-scarred Whitewall Mountain on the opposite side of Zealand Notch. The mountain was denuded decades earlier by logging activity and two great forest fires. Seen at the base of the cliffs is the grade of the former Zealand Valley Railroad. (Courtesy of AMC.)

Lumberman J.E. Henry's Zealand Valley
Railroad operated from 1884 to 1892 and was
responsible for hauling millions of board feet
of timber out of the deep valley separating
the Willey Range from the Little River
Mountains and Zealand Mountain. Hikers
venturing into the Zealand Valley today
continue to follow portions of the old rail
bed. Pictured in this undated photograph
is Locomotive No. 1, the *J.E. Henry.*

The Appalachian Mountain Club's Zealand Falls
Hut rests near the northeastern base of Zealand
Mountain and about 200 feet above Zealand
Pond at the highest point of Zealand Notch.
The hut, seen here at a distance in this Guy
Shorey postcard image from 1936, is flanked
on the left by tumbling Whitewall Brook and
nearby Zealand Falls. (Courtesy of AMC.)

A couple of young hikers rest atop the open summit of 4,902-foot South Twin during an August 1934 excursion to the summit. Pictured alongside the youngsters is a sign for the Twinway Trail, which is the main route between AMC's Galehead Hut at the base of South Twin and Zealand Falls Hut, some seven miles away. The Twinway is also a link in the Appalachian Trail. (Courtesy of AMC.)

Trees encrusted in ice and snow dangle over the narrow path connecting the peaks of North and South Twin in this winter image from the 1920s. The Twins are among the highest peaks outside of the Presidential Range and Franconia Range, with South Twin ranked 9th on the list and North Twin (4,761 feet) ranked 11th.

A few miles north and east of the Twins and due north of Zealand Mountain lies Mount Hale, a 4,054-foot peak that is the highest point of the so-called Little River Mountains. The steel fire lookout tower shown here was erected atop Hale in 1928 and was in service through 1948. Though mostly viewless today due to tree growth, the summit once had a grand view of Mount Washington and many nearby peaks. (Courtesy of WMNF.)

Mount Hale was named for Boston Congregational minister Rev. Everett Edward Hale (1822–1909), author of the classic American short story "A Man without a Country" and an avid White Mountain explorer who frequently joined state geologist Charles T. Jackson during his early forays across the mountains. One of Jackson's successors, Charles Hitchcock, ultimately named the peak in Hale's honor.

Hiker and photographer Clyde Smith took this photograph of Mount Hale and its fire tower in 1929, just a year after it was built. Seen just a short distance below the mostly wooded summit is the roof of the fire lookout's high mountain cabin. (Courtesy of CW.)

A forest fire lookout working atop the tower on Mount Hale in May 1939 tries to site a fire through an alidade, which assisted observers in pinpointing the location of a blaze. In the wake of the devastating September 1938 New England hurricane, which felled hundreds of thousands of trees in the White Mountains, fire observers must have been especially vigilant that spring and summer. (Courtesy of WMNF.)

Galehead Mountain, a conspicuous hump at the eastern end of Garfield Ridge, was raised up to 4,000-Footer status in 1975 when newly revised US Geological Survey maps showed its summit elevation was 4,024 feet and not 3,948 feet, as previously surveyed. The mostly wooded mountain is probably best associated with the AMC hut of the same name. Galehead Hut, shown here in this undated image, was the next-to-last of the club's chain of huts to be built, back in 1932. (Courtesy of AMC.)

Packing in supplies to huts such as AMC's Galehead facility is a time-honored tradition among "croo" members. Here, W. Kent Olsen (left) and Frederic B. Preston (right) are pictured in the summer of 1965 arriving at Galehead Hut with loaded pack boards after a challenging 4.6-mile uphill trek with an elevation gain of about 2,000 feet. Typically, pack board loads will weigh 75 pounds or more. (Courtesy of AMC.)

This is one of the few surviving images of the fire lookout structure that once operated for less than a decade atop 4,500-foot Mount Garfield. Built by Civilian Conservation Corps members, who transported building materials up the mountain on a crude tractor road, the summit outpost was manned from 1940 to 1948. All that remains today of the structure is its square concrete base. (Courtesy of AMC.)

Following the 1881 assassination of Pres. James Garfield (1831–1881), selectmen in the town of Franconia voted to rename one area mountain in honor of the nation's 20th president. Previously known as the Haystack (for its symmetrical shape) and also Hooket, the 4,500-foot peak lies northeast of Mount Lafayette and the peaks of the Franconia Range and was actually a trail-less mountain until 1897.

In 1916, just after completion of the Garfield Ridge Trail linking Mount Lafayette with the Twin Range to the east, an overnight shelter was built near remote Garfield Pond, a small pond about 600 vertical feet below Mount Garfield's summit. Rebuilt several times over the years, the shelter was removed in 1971 after years of overuse. Here, an AMC crew member is seen during a 1940 rebuild of the log structure. (Courtesy of AMC.)

Though there is no longer a trail to it, beautiful Hawthorne Falls on the northeast slopes of Mount Garfield was a frequent destination of hikers in the late 19th and early 20th centuries. Located along Garfield Stream, the secluded waterfall honoring writer Nathaniel Hawthorne was given its name in 1880 by an exploring party led by Bethlehem guide and woodsman Allen "Old Man" Thompson. (Courtesy of AMC.)

196   The Willey House, Crawford Notch, White Mts.

The lower slopes of Mount Willey in Crawford Notch were the scene of one of the region's greatest mountain tragedies. On the night of August 28, 1826, a massive landslide came crashing down Mount Willey's steep east-facing slopes and buried alive members of the Sam Willey family and their two hired hands. The Willeys, who lived in the building shown above, were crushed by the landslide rubble as they tried to flee their home. As chance would have it, the building itself was miraculously spared destruction when two large boulders (below) situated a short distance above and behind the Willey House diverted the track of the slide to either side of the building.

BOULDERS THAT SPLIT THE KILLEY SLIDE, CRAWFORD NOTCH, N. H.

For more than a century, the peaks of the Willey Range were frequently climbed by guests staying at the historic Crawford House at the top of Crawford Notch. The first Crawford House was built in 1852 by Thomas Crawford and its successor just a few years later following an April 1859 fire. In this stereoscopic image from the late 1800s, the upper slopes of Mount Field (4,340 feet) and its subsidiary peak, Mount Avalon, are seen from the front veranda of the hotel.

Though its waters lie nearly 1,500 feet below the summit of Mount Willey (4,285 feet), Ethan Pond has long been associated with the highest peak in the Willey Range. As guidebook author Steven Smith writes, the "pretty lakelet" lies below "the frowning western cliffs of Mount Willey." Here, three hikers are seen paying a visit to the shores of the five-acre pond in August 1936. (Courtesy of AMC.)

Long the bane of peakbagging hikers, remote Owl's Head Mountain lies deep in the heart of the federally designated Pemigewasset Wilderness and remains the lone mountain on the 4,000-Footer list without a maintained trail to its wooded summit. Requiring a long and tiresome nine-mile one-way walk to its 4,025-foot summit, the most popular ascent route includes a climb up the infamous Owl's Head slide on its western-facing slopes.

Lumbering operations throughout the White Mountains were an ongoing concern for much of the late 19th and early 20th centuries. Indiscriminate clear-cutting and catastrophic forest fires like the well-documented 1907 Owl's Head Fire in the central Whites heavily damaged the lower slopes of many of the higher peaks. Ignited by a lightning strike near a remote logging camp, this fire destroyed 30,000 acres of prime forestland. (Courtesy of WMNF.)

The extent of lumbering operations in the Pemigewasset Wilderness during the early 1900s is evident in this near-century-old image of the clear-cut Burnt Brook basin near remote Shoal Pond. Extensive clear-cutting is also visible on the north-facing slopes of the distant 4,000-foot peaks of Mounts Carrigain and Hancock. (Courtesy of WMNF.)

The distant mountain views available from this log landing along Cedar Brook near Mount Hancock reveal the extent of logging activity on the upper slopes of Owl's Head Mountain, seen here in the upper left corner of the image. This photograph is probably from the early 1930s, when timber cutting in the East Branch country was being done by crews of the Parker-Young Company. (Courtesy of UPHS.)

In this remarkable undated aerial photograph of Mount Hancock and its surrounding country, miles of logging tote roads are visible on all sides of the mountain's slopes, with some extending nearly to the crest of the summit ridgeline at an elevation of close to 4,000 feet. In the early 1940s, Mount Hancock and nearby Mount Hitchcock saw some of the last logging activity to take place in the Pemi Wilderness. (Courtesy of AMC.)

JAMES E. HENRY

New Hampshire native James Everell Henry was the region's most famous lumberman, as his logging crews and trains invaded much of the central White Mountains region, including today's Pemigewasset Wilderness area and the secluded Zealand River valley. Remnants of his long-abandoned railroad operations are utilized today as hiking trails to many of the most popular and remote 4,000-Footers.

Four

THE OUTLYING PEAKS

Wild and scenic Carter Notch is squeezed into the mountain landscape between neighboring 4,000-Footers Carter Dome to the east and Wildcat Mountain to the west. The notch is home to a pair of rock-rimmed ponds known as the Carter Lakes. In this undated Guy Shorey postcard, both lakes are visible, along with the former Carter Dome fire lookout's cabin on the shore of Upper Carter Pond. (Courtesy of DG.)

The Carter-Moriah Trail in the eastern White Mountains runs across four peaks on the 4,000-Footer list, including 4,049-foot Mount Moriah, the northernmost peak on the Carter Range. Other peaks on the range include Carter Dome, South Carter, and Middle Carter. This image, taken by Walter James in September 1909, shows the view looking south from Moriah and is taken from the two-volume book *Our Mountain Trips*, published by Bondcliff Books.

In this 1930 image from the upper reaches of the Carter Dome Trail on the east side of Pinkham Notch, the path leads upwards to the 4,832-foot peak of Carter Dome. Visible at the top is a 30-foot steel fire lookout tower constructed by the Forest Service in 1924. The well-constructed path was used to ferry supplies to the summit by saddle horse. (Courtesy of AMC.)

A good portion of the Carter Range and the adjacent Wild River valley to the east sustained heavy damage in a 1903 forest fire covering an estimated 12,000 acres. The lasting damage of the conflagration is seen in this c. 1920 Forest Service image taken along the heights of Carter Dome. Notice the two individuals inspecting the damage in the so-called "skeleton forest." (Courtesy of WMNF.)

During a 1931 visit to Carter Dome, Clyde Smith snapped this image of a US Forest Service fire lookout who has just arrived at his summit post with a backpack load of water and other provisions. The first lookout tower was established atop the mountain in 1907, and from 1913 to 1918, it was operated by the State of New Hampshire. After that, the tower was manned by White Mountain National Forest personnel. (Courtesy of CW.)

Wild Carter Notch provides the dramatic setting for AMC's Carter Notch Hut, one of the oldest in the club's chain of operating mountain huts. The notch, with an elevation of 3,388 feet, is the low point on the ridge between Wildcat Ridge to the west and the Carter Range to the east. As seen in this postcard image, the steep slopes of Wildcat Mountain rear up directly behind the hut. (Courtesy of DG.)

The south shore of Lower Carter Pond is walled in by a line of boulders known as the Ramparts. Guidebook author Steven D. Smith describes the Ramparts as "immense chunks of rock torn from the cliffs of Carter Dome and strewn in a tumbled confusion of stone and scrub." Nineteenth-century guidebook author Moses Sweeter adds that they are "a lofty line of immense bounders . . . affording some of the most remarkable rock-scenery in the mountains."

The major summits near Waterville Valley in the southern White Mountains have been popular with area visitors since the mid-1800s. The region is credited with establishing the first network of hiking trails in the country, and several of these early paths led to the top of 4,340-foot Mount Osceola. Here, trampers on an 1887 outing enjoy the views from along the Mount Osceola Trail. (Courtesy of WV.)

EAST FROM MT OSCEOLA

Despite its relatively modest summit elevation, Osceola affords one of the best mountaintop views in the Whites, with more than 40 of the other 4,000-Footers visible from various locales around the summit. This older, undated postcard shows the view towards the interior of the Pemi Wilderness and distant Mount Washington and the peaks of the Presidential Range. (Courtesy of DG.)

For nearly five decades, beginning in 1910, the summit of Mount Osceola (4,340 feet) near Waterville Valley was the site of an active forest fire lookout tower, first operated by the state and then later by the US Forest Service. The steel tower depicted here was built in 1942 and was last manned in the mid-1950s. It was eventually removed by the US Forest Service in 1985, though its concrete abutments remain on the summit.

The fire lookout working atop Mount Osceola in the mid-1930s spent his off hours in this cabin, located about a half-mile below the summit. This US Forest Service image was taken by photographer Paul S. Carter in January 1935. (Courtesy of WMNF.)

The New England Hurricane of September 21, 1938, left its mark on the Waterville Valley area and, in particular, on Mount Osceola, where there was widespread damage. In this photograph taken a month after the storm, US Forest Service photographer B.W. Muir surveys the damage along the former Breadtray Trail to Osceola. In this instance, the damage was so severe that the trail was closed permanently. (Courtesy of WMNF.)

Another victim of the Hurricane of 1938 was the Greeley Pond Nature Trail, a scenic loop trail that climbed from the Greeley Pond Path in Mad River Notch towards the base of the so-called Painted Cliff on the slopes of East Osceola. This US Forest Service image from January 1935 was taken from a spot along the nature trail where hikers could look down on Upper Greeley Pond. (Courtesy of WMNF.)

Two of the more prominent mountain landmarks in the Waterville Valley area are the great landslides that scar the sides of Mount Tripyramid. An October 1869 rainstorm produced the first so-called "South Slide," while a second South Slide and new "North Slide" were caused by a summer rainstorm in 1885. This image, taken by Edward H. Lorenz, shows the North Slide as it appeared in 1910. (Courtesy of WV.)

From the Waterville Valley side of the mountain, the great North Slide has, for years, been the most popular hiking route up 4,180-foot North Tripyramid. Though steep, rocky, and downright dangerous when wet, the slide offers outstanding views of the region to hikers, such as the hardy souls pictured ascending the mountain in 1988. (Courtesy of AMC.)

From the north and east, the Tripyramids have a distinctly different look, as they are forested from base to summit. This image, taken from the Swift River valley, shows North Tripyramid on the far left and the long ridge extending north and west to the subsidiary summit of Scaur Peak. This is the view that would be most familiar to motorists travelling along the Kancamagus Highway from Conway to Lincoln.

The three angular peaks of Mount Tripyramid anchor the northwest end of the Sandwich Range. All three summits rise above 4,000 feet in elevation, but only the North and Middle summits qualify for inclusion on the AMC peakbagging list. Prior to 1860, the peaks were known as Saddle Mountain, Waterville Haystack, and Passaconaway. Viewed here from North Tripyramid are the Middle (left) and South Peaks. (Courtesy of Steven D. Smith.)

With its extensive band of open ledges on its south-facing upper slopes, it's not hard to figure out how 4,020-foot Mount Whiteface earned its name. The prominent peak in the center of the Sandwich Range was identified as Whiteface as far back as 1784 (by Jeremy Belknap) and again in 1816 by mapmaker Philip Carrigain. The first trail to its south summit was established in the 1850s.

The symmetrical cone of Mount Passaconway (4,043 feet), pictured here from neighboring Mount Potash, is a conspicuous landmark as viewed from the Swift River valley to the north and the Wonalancet lowlands and Lakes Region to the south. Named for the great sachem, or chief, of the Pennacook tribe, the mountain was originally identified on an early map as North Whiteface, but its present name was bestowed upon the peak by state geologist Charles Hitchcock in 1871.

Mount Whiteface is best known for its splendid views from its open south summit, but as this old postcard shows, ample views to the north and towards Mount Washington were also available from the site of the former Camp Heermance shelter. The original shelter was built close by the south summit in 1912 under the direction of trail-building minister Edgar Laing Heermance and was rebuilt two decades later. (Courtesy of DG.)

One of the earliest overnight shelters to be constructed on the Sandwich Range was Passaconaway Lodge, built in 1891 on the east side of the summit cone of Mount Passaconaway at an elevation of approximately 3,500 feet. Over the years, the shelter was rebuilt several times and even renamed Camp Rich after a prominent member of the Wonlancet Out Door Club. This undated postcard probably shows the second shelter located at the site. (Courtesy of DG.)

Sprawling Mount Moosilauke (4,802 feet) is the most dominant landmark in the southwestern White Mountains and one of the most popular hiking destinations among the 4,000-Footers. Moosilauke has a legion of devotees due to its long ties with Dartmouth College. The college, in fact, owns more than 4,500 acres on the east side of the mountain. This view shows the mountain as seen from nearby Pike, New Hampshire. (Courtesy of DG.)

Mount Moosilauke probably has as storied a history as any White Mountain peak other than Mount Washington. It was first visited as early as 1773 by local moose hunter Chase Whitcher, and during the winter of 1869–1870, its summit was occupied for two months as a trial run for a planned winter stay atop Mount Washington the following year. In this stereoscopic image, one of the winter occupants is shown hauling a load of firewood up to the Summit House.

THURSDAY, JANUARY 15, 1942   IN THE WHITE MOUNTAINS   PRICE — SIX CEN

Give
Bonds

Two Killed, Five Injured In Bomber Crash On Mt. Moosilauke Last Night

ABOUT 100 ATTEND WHITEFIELD FIRST AID

About 100 from the Whitefield Red Cross chapter area, which includes Carroll, Dalton and Jefferson in addition to Whitefield gathered at Whitefield town hall on Tuesday night for the first lesson of the series in first aid. Mrs. Nellie Marshall and Mrs. Mary Rogers of Jefferson were the instructors. Due to other demands, the second class will not meet until Tuesday, January 20.

Winter Sports Calendar
Jan. 17—Jefferson Sports Meet.
Jan. 24—Groveton Sports Meet.
Jan. 31—Lisbon Sports Meet.
Feb. 7—Littleton Sports Meet.
Feb. 11—Woodsville Sports Meet.
Feb. 14—Lancaster Sports Meet.
Feb. 21—Whitefield Sports Meet.
Mar. 7—Franconia Sports Meet. (tent.)

Explosions Heard In Lincoln, North Woodstock

Rescuers Tramp Five Miles into Wilderness High On Mountain to Bring Five of Seven Fliers to Lincoln Hospital—Report Three Bombs Explode

Two men were killed and five narrowly missed death when a bomber described as a Douglas B-18 crashed on Mt. Moosilauke between North Woodstock and Warren, last night.

It was reported that the big plane was loaded with four bombs, three of which exploded to shake the countryside for miles around. Another version was that the gas tanks may have exploded.

Working feverishly all night, a crew of more than 50 volunteer searchers, including experienced...

Announce New Appointees In Lisbon Defense Set-Up

Mrs. Lionel Pechey to Head Control Center Staff—
Boy Scouts Plan to Collect Newspapers, Magazines

The horrors of World War II struck very close to home in January 1942, when a B-18 bomber on submarine patrol lost its way in a snowstorm and smashed into the east side of the mountain outside North Woodstock, New Hampshire. Though two crewmen were killed, the remaining five members miraculously survived the crash and were rescued during a heroic overnight effort involving both military and civilian personnel.

The B-18 crash site remains a popular destination for many hikers each year. Though there's no official path to the site, a well-flagged route can be followed. In this image taken by the author during a May 1990 visit to the crash site on Mount Waternomee, a subsidiary peak of Mount Moosilauke, a curious hiker examines the wreckage of the bomber.

One of only two 4,000-Footers located north of US Route 2, Mount Waumbek (4,006 feet) is the highest point along the Pliny Range, which runs from the Israel River valley near Jefferson north to the wild and remote Kilkenny region. Though hikers have been visiting the wooded summit for years, there was no officially maintained path to the mountaintop until the 1970s. In this image from the early 1900s, Waumbek is seen from Bray Hill in neighboring Whitefield.

Much like its neighbor to the south, 4,170-foot Mount Cabot has a wooded, viewless summit, but visitors should not despair. There are several nice outlooks on the way up the mountain, including one from the site of a former fire tower about a half-mile below the true summit. Here is an image of the old fire warden's cabin on Cabot as it appeared in the late 1920s. (Courtesy of CW.)

Five

SUMMIT AND BACKCOUNTRY STRUCTURES

Man-made structures have dotted the upper reaches of the White Mountains for more than a century and a half. Summit hotels, backcountry shelters, and the Appalachian Mountain Club's string of mountain huts have all played a role in the region's long and storied history. Here, construction crews under the direction of Clarence Buzzell of Randolph pose for a photograph in front of the new Lakes of the Clouds Hut, which opened in 1915. (Courtesy of DG.)

On June 30, 1900, AMC members William Curtis and Allen Ormsbee were hiking to a club gathering at Mount Washington's summit when they were caught by a fierce storm that would claim both their lives. In response to this tragic event, a small wood-frame emergency refuge was built the following year at the base of Mount Monroe, not far from where Curtis perished. The refuge was supposed to be used only in the event of a true emergency situation, but pleasure camping became more common at the site as hikers sought shelter above treeline. With newer and larger accommodations an obvious necessity, AMC built a new stone hut in the same general area, and in its first year of operation (1915), more than 225 guests overnighted at the new Lakes of the Clouds facility. (Both, courtesy of AMC.)

Over the course of more than 100 years, beginning in 1853, Mount Washington was home to three different Summit House hotels. The second Summit House, pictured here, was built atop Mount Washington in 1872–1873 with construction materials hauled up the mountain by the recently opened Cog Railway. At full build-out, it could accommodate as many as 200 seasonal patrons, and among its many guests were two US presidents, author Harriet Beecher Stowe, circus man P.T. Barnum, and former Union army general George McClellan.

The third and last Mount Washington Summit House was built in 1914–1915 and served as a replacement for the second Summit House, which burned to the ground in a June 1908 summit fire. This prefabricated wooden structure, primarily built in the Lisbon, New Hampshire, shops of Sylvanus Morgan, accommodated as many as 90 overnight guests. The building was torn down in 1980 after completion of the current state-owned Sherman Adams Summit Building.

Among the earliest structures atop Mount Washington was the Tip-Top House, built at the same time as the first Summit House in 1853. While its stone foundation consisted of rocks culled from the mountain itself, all timber and boards had to be hauled up the mountain by horse from a mill in nearby Jefferson. Originally, it was a flat-roofed building, with the pitched roof shown here added in the early 1860s.

The Tip-Top House never rivaled the later second and third Summit Houses in terms of comfort or splendor, but the squat structure welcomed many a Mount Washington visitor in its day. This early photograph shows the interior of the building, with sitting chairs, a warming stove, and what looks like a well-stocked bar.

Another of Mount Washington's many claims to fame is that it was once home to the only mountaintop newspaper in the country, if not the world. *Among the Clouds*, founded in 1877 by Henry M. Burt, was published daily atop the mountain during the busy summer tourist season. For the first seven years of operation, it was housed in the Tip-Top House. A summit building of its own, pictured here, was built and opened in 1884. (Courtesy of MWO.)

HENRY M. BURT.

Henry Burt, founder and longtime editor and publisher of *Among the Clouds*, got the inspiration to establish the newspaper during an 1874 visit to the mountain when he was stormbound in the Summit House. For more than 30 summers, the paper reported on the news from the summit and other area hotels and might have continued on but for the June 1908 fire that destroyed the paper's summit offices.

During its long existence, the Mount Washington Cog Railway has seen many different structures built along its right of way. This undated image shows the Half Way Shelter House, situated about one and a half miles from the base station at Marshfield. The planking alongside the tracks indicates this was probably a transfer platform where riders would disembark from one train and hop onto another for the trip either up or down the mountain.

On the opposite side of Mount Washington, along the Carriage Road, stood the better-known Halfway House. The original structure, shown here, was built at the same time that the road was under construction in the mid-1850s. It offered shelter not just to construction workers but also to mountain adventurers caught in poor weather. It was entirely rebuilt after the Carriage Road opened to the public and gained more popularity.

Hermit Lake Shelter, at the base of Mount Washington's spectacular Tuckerman Ravine, was built by AMC in 1921 and replaced a previous camp established there by the club. Located on the eastern shore of the lake, the unfurnished, open log structure, pictured here in 1939, had room for 10 overnight visitors. In the mid-1930s, a second shelter was added on the northwest shore of the lake. (Courtesy of WMNF.)

To accommodate the growing number of visitors to Tuckerman Ravine, especially during the spring ski season, the US Forest Service, with assistance from the Civilian Conservation Corps, erected the first Tuckerman Ravine Shelter in 1937. The 2,000-square-foot building was a popular gathering place, offering warmth, shelter, and first aid. It was destroyed by fire in 1951, while a smaller replacement building met the same fate in 1972. (Courtesy of WMNF.)

The Appalachian Mountain Club's Carter Notch Hut is the oldest standing facility in the club's famed White Mountains hut system. The stone structure dates back to 1914, was built to replace a small log cabin constructed a decade earlier, and was known as Carter Notch Camp. Visible in the interior view below are a wood cookstove, various pots and pans, dinnerware, a kerosene lamp, and a fold-down metal bunk. An earlier club history of the AMC hut system, compiled by Chris Stewart and Mike Torrey, notes that "the main room of the hut served as a bunkroom, kitchen, dining room, and crew quarters."

As evidenced in the two images appearing on this page, the earliest days of fire protection efforts in the Whites were rudimentary at best, at least in terms of available physical structures. In the image to the right, taken in 1905, two summit visitors to Carter Dome stand atop a crude observation tower built by local woodsmen and undoubtedly utilized by both fire lookouts and hikers. In subsequent years, three bigger and better fire towers would grace the summit of Carter Dome, including a 30-foot steel tower erected in 1924 and eventually removed in 1947. In the photograph above, also from 1905, the summit fire lookout, identified only as "Neal the Fire Warden," takes a break at his primitive mountaintop shelter. (Both, courtesy of AMC.)

The construction of the Appalachian Mountain Club's Mizpah Spring Hut in 1964 marked the completion of AMC's chain of high mountain huts spread across the White Mountains. Replacing a former rustic shelter at the site, the new hut at the base of the southwest summit of Mount Pierce was formally dedicated in the ceremony pictured above on July 10, 1965. In the photograph below, taken in 1934, an unidentified man addresses a group of hikers outside the former Mizpah Spring Shelter. This log structure was built in 1915 after AMC had extended the existing Webster Cliff Trail from Mount Jackson to Mount Pierce by way of Mizpah Spring. (Below, courtesy of AMC.)

For more than 80 years, the broad, flat, open summit of Mount Moosilauke was occupied by a seasonally operated hotel. The original summit hotel was a 30-by-15-foot stone structure that opened to great fanfare on July 4, 1860. Variously known as the Prospect House, Summit House, and Tip-Top House, the hotel was expanded several times through the years. Seen here are the original building on the right and, on the left, a large addition built in 1872.

In 1933, Dartmouth College purchased more than 900 acres of forestland on Mount Moosilauke and soon thereafter converted an old horse stable on its holdings into its first Ravine Camp. After fire destroyed that building in 1935, a second camp was constructed at the base of Gorge Brook. Called Ravine Lodge, it opened in 1939 and was built out of virgin spruce cut on site. The lodge has since been replaced by a new, modern facility.

The Appalachian Mountain Club's Galehead Hut, seen here in 1936, was built under the direction of legendary AMC hutmaster Joe Dodge at a cost of $10,527.98. It sat a half-mile below Galehead Mountain's summit and a steep 0.8 mile below the summit of nearby South Twin. After the original hut was razed, a new Galehead Hut was built and opened in 2000. (Courtesy of DG.)

Two young hikers are pictured here taking a break at Garfield Pond Shelter in the summer of 1934. As noted previously, this second log shelter at the site was built in 1925. It stayed in service until the early 1970s, when overuse prompted WMNF officials to remove the shelter and replace it with the new Garfield Ridge Shelter about a mile away along the Garfield Ridge Trail. (Courtesy of AMC.)

Six

HIKING AND SKIING THE 4,000-FOOTERS

The White Mountain National Forest and its highest peaks have been attracting visitors for more than two centuries. These include recreational hikers and backpackers, downhill and backcountry skiers, and research scientists, among others. In this image from 1931, three members of a Boy Scout group are seen packing supplies along the lower reaches of the Valley Way Trail in the Northern Presidential Range. (Courtesy of WMNF.)

From left to right, trampers Harriet "Hattie" Freeman, Edith Hull, Emma Cummings, and Fred Freeman enjoy the view from a trail bridge during a weeklong 1902 hike along the Presidential Range. Their adventure, which inspired them to work for permanent preservation of the White Mountains, was recently chronicled in the book *Glorious Mountain Days*, by Allison Bell and Maida Goodwin, published in 2018. (Courtesy of RMC.)

In 1931, the US Forest Service enlisted the help of these Boy Scouts to undertake a trail improvement project along the Valley Way Trail, which leads from Randolph up to AMC's Madison Spring Hut. The Scouts are pictured at their campsite with WMNF district ranger Truman Hale. (Courtesy of WMNF.)

Pack boy Clyde Smith, pictured here in 1928, is loaded down with mattresses and a bag of sand as he ferries supplies to AMC's Madison Spring Hut. His load weighed an impressive 130 pounds. (Courtesy of CW.)

Trudging up a steep mountain trail can be grueling work, but the experience can also be fun, as these unidentified Waterville Valley hikers wage a playful tug of war on the gravelly South Slide of Mount Tripyramid. (Courtesy of WV.)

Clyde Smith, right, and a trail companion take a break along an open stretch of the Carter Dome Trail near Pinkham Notch with Mount Hight rising up behind them. Smith was part of a trail crew that spent much of the summer of 1926 working to improve the trail, which also served as a tractor road to the fire tower at the summit of Carter Dome. (Courtesy of CW.)

The father-and-son team of Peter (left) and Roger Doucette (right) take a well-earned break as they work their way up the so-called "Cedar Brook Slide" on the northwest slope of Mount Hancock in May 1995. Hikers bound for Hancock's wooded and trailless northwest summit frequently ascend the mountain by way of this slide, which occurred during a massive rain event in November 1927.

On Columbus Day weekend in October 1990, this Pennsylvania couple hiked nearly nine miles (one way) from the Kancamagus Highway in Lincoln to the summit of Bondcliff to exchange wedding vows in a unique mountaintop ceremony. Howard Feist (left) and Susan Wonsik were officially wed by local justice of the peace Jane Duguay. Not surprising, there were no other members of the couple's wedding party.

Reaching all the 4,000-Footers is a year-round pursuit for many hikers, and finishing the list in winter is a particularly rewarding experience. For Lexington, Massachusetts, hiker Larry Labonte, pictured here on the right, March 19, 1995, is a day he will always remember. His successful ascent of Mount Jefferson that day came 14 months after he nearly lost both feet to frostbite after getting lost on a midwinter hike up Mount Pierce. Here, Labonte holds up a banner recognizing Dr. Harry McDade and the staff of Littleton Regional Hospital for their feet-saving medical care. At left is fellow hiker Guy Jubinville. (Courtesy of Larry Labonte.)

Longtime White Mountain peakbagging guru Eugene Daniell is pictured here with his wife, Debi Clark, at the summit of Mount Adams in May 1983. The hike marked the completion of Clark's effort to bag all 48 of the White Mountain 4,000-Footers, a feat her husband accomplished at least a dozen times in his long hiking career. (Courtesy of Debi Clark.)

4000-FOOTER CLUB OF THE WHITE MOUNTAINS
APPALACHIAN MOUNTAIN CLUB

I have climbed to the summits of all the official peaks of the 4000-Footer Club of the White Mountains

Committee

Approved

President

Copyright 1958 Appalachian Mt. Club

Since the list of peaks was compiled by AMC in 1957, thousands of hikers have undertaken the challenge of climbing to the summits of New Hampshire's 48 official 4,000-foot summits. For most folks, it takes several years to bag all the summits, as was the case with the author of this book, who climbed his first peak (Osceola) in July 1982 and his final one (Bondcliff) in August 1987. Here is his official AMC Four Thousand Footer Club scroll.

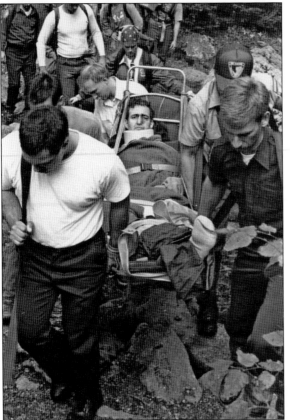

Accidents, injuries, and occasional deaths have long been associated with the 4,000-Footers, and none more so than Mount Washington, where more than 150 lives have been lost since 1849, when Englishman Frederick Strickland became the first person to die on the mountain. Fortunately, most accidents on Mount Washington and elsewhere in the Whites are not fatal, as was the case back in September 1988, when Massachusetts hiker Paul Singley received serious but nonfatal injuries when he wandered off-trail and tumbled 30 feet down a streambed in the mountain's rugged Ammonoosuc Ravine. Specialized technical rescue teams, using ropes, had to first litter a suspended Singley safely over and across Gem Pool. They then had to carry him more than a mile over rough, rocky terrain to a waiting ambulance at the Cog Railway base station, all while the 34-year-old man was suffering from multiple broken ribs, a broken leg, and one punctured lung.

For a handful of the White Mountain 4,000-Footers, downhill skiing has been as much a part of their history as hiking or mountain climbing. Three of the high peaks—Cannon, Tecumseh, and Wildcat—have developed ski areas, while Mount Washington and Mount Moosilauke are steeped in New England ski lore. Pictured here is the Richard Taft Ski Trail on Cannon Mountain, one of the earliest racing trails in the country and the first in New England cut specially for downhill racing. Work on the trail began in 1932, and with the aid of the newly formed Civilian Conservation Corps, it was finished in time for the winter season of 1933–1934. According to a ski guide from the late 1930s, the Taft Trail ran slightly longer than two miles with an elevation drop of 2,100 feet and a maximum grade of 34 percent. "A wide variety of turns lend excitement," gushed the guide. (Courtesy of CW.)

Due to its prime location in Franconia Notch, Cannon's wide-open ski terrain offers superb views of the surrounding mountains, including snow-capped Mount Lafayette and the peaks along nearby Franconia Ridge. The mountain remains the lone ski area to be operated by the state and is well known for its challenging runs.

In this US Forest Service image from 1938, the upper part of the Taft Trail is shown from near the mountain's summit. This part of the trail was known as the Taft Slalom Trail, while the lower section below the small peak seen here was called the Taft Race Trail. Portions of this trail were later incorporated into the former Mittersill ski area, which operated on the lower slopes of Cannon's sub-peak once known as Mount Jackson. (Courtesy of WMNF.)

The eyes of the international ski world were focused on Cannon Mountain in March 1967, when the newly established World Cup ski circuit descended upon Franconia Notch for a pair of races featuring some of the best skiers in the world. International ski sensation Jean-Claude Killy (right) of France cemented his reputation as the top skier on the circuit with back-to-back wins in downhill and giant slalom competitions. The World Cup event, the first ever held on American soil, drew thousands of spectators to the mountain, including many old-time Cannon ski veterans. It was also televised live to the nation by CBS Sports and brought much acclaim to the relatively small New England ski mountain. (Below, courtesy of NESM.)

The Pinkham Notch area in the eastern White Mountains has been a magnet for skiers for almost a century now. The great glacial ravines on Mount Washington's east-facing slopes have long been a draw for hardcore backcountry skiers, while just a few miles north of the AMC Pinkham Notch Camp along Route 16 lies the popular Wildcat Mountain Ski Area.

Starting with the 1936 winter season, a small ski slope was developed on the lower slopes of Wildcat Mountain directly across from AMC's Pinkham Notch Camp. Often referred to as the Pinkham Notch Practice Slope, it was especially popular with beginner skiers and was an easy hike from the nearby AMC camp. It was in existence for just a few years and is now entirely reforested. (Courtesy of WMNF.)

Along with its two official 4,000-foot summits, Wildcat Mountain is home to one of the most challenging downhill ski areas in New England. Ski development on Wildcat began in the 1930s, when the CCC cut one of the nation's earliest racing trails. This, in turn, led to the eventual development of Wildcat Mountain Ski Area and the installation of the nation's first base-to-summit gondola in 1958. The aerial photograph above, taken in 1962, shows Wildcat and its ski slopes along with the adjoining peaks of the Carter Range just to the north. At right, a skier makes his way down one of Wildcat's ski runs in 1958. The scene is virtually unchanged today, as the mountain's special use permit from the White Mountain National Forest restricts development at its base area. Though frustrating at the time for the ski area's operators, its lack of base area development remains one of its charms with today's skiers. (Above, courtesy of WMNF; right, courtesy of NESM.)

Mount Washington's Tuckerman Ravine and its awe-inspiring headwall have long been a mecca for backcountry skiers. For several generations now, hiking into the ravine and taking on the steep headwall has served as a rite of passage for hardy skiers young and old alike. It was not until the State of New Hampshire opened the road between Jackson and Gorham to year-round traffic that skiing really caught on at Mount Washington. Ease of accessibility, and the 1927 opening of AMC's Pinkham Notch Camp, combined to make Tuck's a true ski destination. Above, the first giant slalom race in the United States the Franklin Edson Memorial Race—was held on April 4, 1937. Below, hundreds of skiers and spectators are on hand for another day of racing. (Above, courtesy of NESM; below, courtesy of DG.)

W. H. POTE.

The spring ski season on Mount Washington's eastern snowfields appears to be coming to a close in this May 1965 image by well-known Granite State photographer Dick Smith. In a good snow year, the spring ski season can last well into June in certain areas of the mountain's ravines. (Courtesy of WMNF.)

Judging by the number of vehicles parked along the Pinkham Notch Road in this March 10, 1940, photograph, there is no shortage of late-winter skiers headed for some backcountry skiing on Mount Washington. The cars are parked near AMC's Pinkham Notch Camp at the eastern base of the mountain. (Courtesy of WMNF.)

The first-ever downhill ski race in the United States took place on another New Hampshire 4,000-Footer, Mount Moosilauke, in the southwestern White Mountains. Dartmouth College ski coach Anton Diettrich is credited with introducing the idea of holding a ski race on the Mount Moosilauke carriage road, and the first such race was conducted in March 1927 over a five-mile course that began near the mountain's South Peak. The winner of this inaugural race was Charles Proctor, with a winning time of 21 minutes. The photograph shown here is from the 1929 event. A film made of the 1932 race by John McCrillis helped convince the National Ski Association to include downhill racing in its competition schedule, and the first National Downhill Championships were held on the Moosilauke carriage road in 1933. (Photograph by Harold H. Leich, courtesy of Jeff Leich.)

Since 1966, Mount Tecumseh (4,003 feet) has been the home of Waterville Valley Ski Resort, one of New Hampshire's and New England's largest ski areas. Opened by the Waterville Company and headed by former US Olympic skier Tom Corcoran (pictured at right), the resort opened in December 1966 with 4 double chairlifts, 18 runs, and a vertical drop of just over 2,000 feet. Sel Hannah, another former Olympian and a well-known ski area designer, was hired to lay out these early trails. Today, the ski area boasts more than 60 trails on 265 skiable acres, with 11 operating lifts. (Both, courtesy of WVR.)

Mount Tecumseh's ski roots go back to the early 1930s, when crews from a nearby Civilian Conservation Corps camp cut what is usually called the Old Tecumseh Ski Trail. This steep and challenging course followed, in part, an existing hiking trail and old logging roads. By 1936, an old logging camp along the route of the trail was converted into the ski cabin shown above. (Courtesy of DG.)

Waterville Valley Ski Resort is known internationally and, over the years, has been home to a dozen World Cup ski races. The first World Cup events were held in 1969, and the mountain was a regular venue on the men's and women's circuit into the 1980s. Pictured here is Austrian skier Roswitha Steiner competing in a 1986 World Cup event at Waterville. (Photograph by Dorothy I. Crossley, courtesy of NESM.)

For a number of years beginning in the mid-1930s, a long, three-mile ski run existed on the western slopes of Mount Kinsman. The Kinsman Ski Trail ran from Kinsman Ridge north of the main summits to the Franconia-Easton Road. Its lower section followed an existing hiking trail, while its upper section was cut through the forest by CCC crews. "It is sporty, with many sudden pitches which keep the skier alert," noted a 1939 ski guide. (Courtesy of WMNF.)

A quartet of ski enthusiasts is about to embark from the AMC Pinkham Notch Camp on an overnight ski trek into the mountains in this image from 1938. Besides carrying their ski equipment, these guys are also loaded down with bulky sleeping gear and provisions for the next few days. (Courtesy of WMNF.)

Spring hiking in the Presidential Range comes with certain risks, as AMC member Stanley Ostrosky discovered in June 1910. He is pictured here after taking a tumble while attempting to cross a snowfield in the Great Gulf. Based on the reaction of his hiking companion, it appears the fall was none too serious and even worthy of a few laughs. (Courtesy of AMC.)

Spectators and skiers attending a downhill ski race on Mount Washington in April 1937 appear to be enjoying the expansive view across Pinkham Notch toward the Carter Range. This image was taken from the Little Headwall at Tuckerman Ravine. (Courtesy of WMNF.)

Beginning in 1882, the Snow-Shoe Section of the Appalachian Mountain Club regularly organized winter excursions into the mountains, often gathering for a week or more each year in Jackson, Gorham, or Waterville Valley. While many of these hikes took them to lesser summits, occasional trips to a 4,000-Footer were undertaken. In the image to the right, two AMC Snow-Shoe Section members stand atop snowbound Mount Tripyramid in late February 1898. Using the Elliott House in Waterville Valley as their base, AMC hikers also paid visits that week to Mounts Osceola, Tecumseh, and nearby Sandwich Dome. Below, two participants in an ambitious January 1905 trek inspect some rime ice at the summit of Mount Washington. This particular trip also included a partial traverse of the Northern Presidentials and an eventual descent to the Ravine House in Randolph. When the winter hikers awoke that morning in Gorham, the temperature was a bone-chilling 16 degrees below zero. (Both, courtesy of AMC.)

Climbing the 4,000-Footers in winter has become an increasingly popular peakbagging pursuit in recent years, but that has not always been the case. From 1960 to 1990, there were less than 150 winter finishers. In the ensuing 30 years, 750 hikers have finished the list. The above photograph depicts the author (far right) heading to his last winter summit in March 1989. Also pictured are Roger Doucette (left) and Creston Ruiter.

The winter of 1925–1926 saw a first-of-its-kind visit to the top of New England when a dog sled team of Alaskan huskies ascended Mount Washington's snow-packed, icy Auto Road. Arthur Walden's dog team made the trip on March 30, 1926, after several years of planning. The team contended with high snowdrifts and winds close to hurricane force but successfully made it to the summit early in the afternoon. (Courtesy of MWO.)

Seven

PEAKBAGGERS AND PIONEERS

Among the nearly 16,000 hikers who have successfully climbed all the New Hampshire 4,000-Footers is former governor Meldrim Thomson of Orford, pictured here leading a party of hikers up Mount Washington on July 1, 1978, the date of the official ground breaking for the mountain's new Sherman Adams summit building. Just two months later, on August 2, 1978, Governor Thomson made the ascent of Mount Liberty to complete his 4,000-Footer quest.

Ulysses S. Grant, the decorated Civil War general of the Union army and later the nation's 18th president, can also lay claim to being the first US chief executive to visit a New Hampshire 4,000-Footer while actually in office. During an August 1869 visit to the White Mountains, Grant, his wife, and their son Jesse rode the newly opened Cog Railway to the summit of Mount Washington, where the president and his entourage were greeted with a cannon salute. President Grant was also met at the mountain by the Cog's founder, Sylvester Marsh, and about 200 visitors gathered atop the Rock Pile to meet the president's train. The above image shows the train that the Grants rode to the mountaintop on August 27, 1869, though it is next to impossible to pick the president out of the assembled crowd. (Left, courtesy of MWO.)

The second sitting president to visit Mount Washington was Rutherford B. Hayes, right, who also ascended via the Cog Railway on Monday, August 20, 1877. For the nation's 19th president, it was not his first visit to the summit. In fact, he'd been atop the mountain four previous times, including once when he was just 11 years old. During his 1877 presidential visit, Hayes was accompanied by his wife and two sons, and while at the summit, he paid a visit to the Signal Station (above), a weather observatory maintained by the US Signal Service. According to Mount Washington historian F. Allen Burt, the sergeant in charge of the Signal Station handed Hayes a telegram from the chief signal officer in Washington. It read, "The Signal Service welcomes the President to the highest office (mountain) save one in the United States."

As noted previously, personnel for the Civilian Conservation Corps played a major role in the early development of downhill skiing in the Whites. CCC crews also worked on a number of major hiking trails and helped construct several Forest Service roads throughout the mountains. In this image from the 1930s, a crew from the CCC uses hand tools to clear a new ski trail at Cannon Mountain. (Courtesy of NESM.)

Former US Supreme Court associate justice William O. Douglas was a nationally known individual who left his mark on the high peaks of the White Mountains. The Minnesota native, who served on the court from 1939 to 1975, was a strong advocate for the outdoors, and his August 1961 *National Geographic* article, "The Friendly Huts of the White Mountains," spurred immense new interest in the venerable AMC hut system.

One of the earliest hiking tragedies to occur in the White Mountains was the unfortunate death of Lizzie Bourne of Kennebunk, Maine. The 23-year-old Bourne perished on the upper slopes of Mount Washington on the night of September 13, 1855, after she collapsed from exhaustion at the end of a grueling ascent of the mountain. Bourne's hiking party, which also included her uncle, aunt, and cousin, were caught in deteriorating weather conditions as they neared the summit, and all were eventually overcome by darkness, high winds, and heavy fog. When Lizzie could no longer continue on, the party sought whatever protection from the elements they could find, but it was not enough to prevent Bourne from succumbing to the conditions. The following morning, after the fog had cleared, it was revealed that Bourne had died just a few hundred yards from the safety and warmth of the Summit House. The marker seen below shows the location where she perished.

Lizzie Bourne's Monument, Mt. Washington.

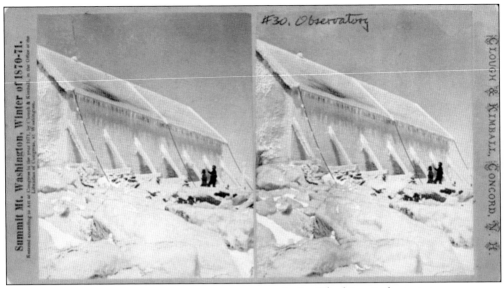

#30. Observatory

CLOUGH & KIMBALL, CONCORD, N.H.

JOSHUA H. HUNTINGTON.

The historic first winter occupation of Mount Washington commenced in November 1870 when Joshua Huntington of Hanover, a veteran of the previous winter's occupation of Mount Moosilauke, climbed the mountain and began taking and recording meteorological observations. Huntington was later joined on the summit by photographers Amos Clough of Warren and Howard A. Kimball of Concord, S.A. Morse of Georgetown, Massachusetts, and Sgt. Theodore Smith of the US Signal Service. The stereoscopic view above is one of a series that was produced and subsequently published by Kimball and Clough. Pictured to the left is Joshua Huntington, whose White Mountain résumé included the consecutive winter occupancies of Mounts Moosilauke and Washington and service as a chief assistant geologist for Charles Hitchcock's expansive and groundbreaking geological survey of the state of New Hampshire, including the White Mountains. (Above, courtesy of MWO.)

Members of the 1870–1871 winter occupation crew atop Mount Washington pose for a group shot near the summit. Pictured from left to right are (first row) Theodore Smith, Amos Clough, and Joshua Huntington; (second row) S.A. Nelson and Howard A. Kimball. Their day-to-day experiences atop the mountain were chronicled in the book *Mount Washington in Winter*, published in 1871. (Courtesy of MWO.)

Due to the success of the first winter occupation of the mountain, the US Signal Service, a branch of the US Army, took over the summit weather observatory the following year and would retain a presence on the mountain until 1887. Among their ranks was Sgt. Winfield Scott Jewell of Lisbon, who served at the station from 1878 to 1880. The Jewell Trail on the western slopes of the mountain is named in his honor. The accompanying photograph shows the interior of the Signal Station as it appeared in January 1880.

119

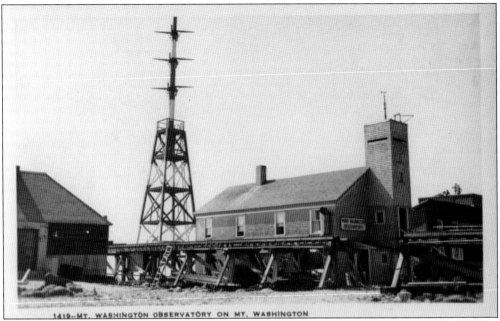

1419..MT. WASHINGTON OBSERVATORY ON MT. WASHINGTON

Mount Washington's long tradition of hosting year-round weather observers was rekindled in 1932 with the establishment of the Mount Washington Observatory. Decades after the last Signal Service officers left the mountain, this new breed of observers began working atop the summit in October 1932. Pictured here is the new observatory building constructed in 1937. Previous to that, the observatory was housed in the old summit Stage Office and the mountaintop Camden Cottage.

On October 14, 1932, the first day of the winter reoccupation of the summit, observatory staffers needed three vehicles to haul their supplies up to the summit. The small convoy of two trucks and one car seen here on a water stop at the Auto Road's Halfway House. Note the ice-covered barrels in the foreground. (Courtesy of MWO.)

For more than 60 years, Mount Washington held the world record for the highest wind gust ever recorded on the surface of the Earth. It was on April 12, 1934, that Mount Washington Observatory staffers recorded a gust of 231 miles an hour during a freak spring wind storm. Observers present at the time of the world record wind were, from left to right, Sal Pagliuca, Alex McKenzie, and Wendell Stephenson. (Courtesy MWO.)

Wild weather notwithstanding, Mount Washington Observatory staff enjoyed some light moments atop the mountain. In this image captured by Melrose, Massachusetts, photographer Harold Orne, MWO staffer Alex McKenzie is seen taking a bath while perusing through the pages of the September 27, 1937, issue of Life magazine. Featured on the cover of the issue is popular singer and actor Nelson Eddy. (Courtesy of MWO.)

Two of the most influential White Mountain hikers of the late 20th century were Guy and Laura Waterman of East Corinth, Vermont. The Watermans were enthusiastic hikers and climbers while also ardent conservationists and prolific writers and historians. For many years, the pair could be frequently found atop Mount Lafayette and along Franconia Ridge, where they worked to preserve the fragile alpine vegetation found along the ridge. They also served as de facto alpine stewards, passing along their acquired knowledge and concerns to thousands of passing hikers. Among their best-known books are *Forest and Crag*, a monumental history of hiking and trailblazing in the Northeast; *Yankee Rock and Ice*, a regional history of rock and ice climbing; and the companion volumes *Backwoods Ethics* and *Wilderness Ethics*. (Above, courtesy of Laura Waterman; left, courtesy of Steven D. Smith.)

For nearly three decades, New Hampshire native Eugene Daniell III (1947–2019) was the poster child for peakbagging in the White Mountains. The tireless Daniell was the first hiker to climb all of the forty-eight 4,000-Footers in each calendar month. He was also a longtime member of the AMC's Four Thousand Footer Committee, serving many years as corresponding secretary, editor of the revered *AMC White Mountain Guide* from 1982 to 2007, and for a number of years, accidents editor for the club's journal, *Appalachia*. Not surprisingly, Daniell produced an entire family of peakbagging hikers, including his daughter, Karen (right), seen here with her dad on a November 1989 hike up Mount Tripyramid. (Both, courtesy of Debi Clark.)

Edward Charles Pickering (1858–1938), seen here on the left in March 1906 while on a snowshoe outing, was a founding member of the Appalachian Mountain Club and served as the club's first president. The Boston-based organization and its ambitious members played a key role in the development of the White Mountain region's vast trail system, which includes sanctioned footpaths to all but one of the 4,000-Footers. (Courtesy of AMC.)

Nathaniel Goodrich, a longtime Dartmouth College librarian and avid outdoorsman, is credited with compiling the first White Mountains 4,000-Footer peakbagging list. His list of 36 peaks first appeared in the December 1931 issue of *Appalachia*, journal of the Appalachian Mountain Club. The list was later revised and currently includes 48 White Mountain summits. Goodrich is pictured here in 1903 near Greeley Ponds at the base of Mount Osceola. (Courtesy of WV.)

During the late 19th century, when established mountain trails were few and far between on the highest peaks, guides such as Vyron Lowe of Randolph were frequently hired to accompany hikers. Vyron was the son of Charles Lowe, a well-known guide and trail builder in his own right. Vyron's two brothers, Charley and Thaddeus, were also mountain guides and trail builders. At right, Vyron Lowe is pictured at The Perch, a private camp on the upper slopes of Mount Adams, along with one of his clients, Emma Cummings. This was during a weeklong tramp across the Presidential Range in July 1902. Below, the trampers take a lunch break in Tuckerman Ravine during the same 1902 hike. Pictured from left to right are Edith Hull, Vyron Lowe, Emma Cummings, and Frederic Freeman. (Both, courtesy of RMC.)

American poet Robert Frost (1874–1963) never wrote a poem about the highest summits of the White Mountains, but during his five years (1915–1920) as a resident of Franconia, he was no stranger to some of the local 4,000-Footers. Author David Tatham, in his book *Robert Frost's White Mountains*, says Frost and his children "tackled Liberty, Lincoln, Moosilauke, the Kinsmans, and others." Among these other favorites was Mount Lafayette. From his small farmhouse on Ore Hill in Franconia, Frost enjoyed a splendid view of the peaks of nearby Franconia Notch, Mounts Garfield and North Twin, and the more distant Presidential Range. Pictured above near his Franconia farmhouse in 1916 is the four-time Pulitzer Prize winner and his son Carol, with Mounts Lafayette and Cannon visible in the background. Below is the Frost homestead in Franconia as it appears today. (Above, courtesy of Rauner Special Collections Library, Dartmouth College.)

Robert and Miriam Underhill were world-class mountaineers who were also frequent visitors to New Hampshire's White Mountains. From their mountain home in Randolph, the Underhills were among the first to complete the 4,000-Footer list in September 1957. Taking things even further, the Underhills next took on the high peaks in calendar winter, and on December 23, 1960, they were the first to complete the winter list when they summited frigid 5,716-foot Mount Jefferson. (Courtesy of AMC.)

While serving as New Hampshire state geologist from 1868 to 1878, Charles Henry Hitchcock oversaw the first statewide geological survey of the state. This multi-year effort, which resulted in the publication of the massive three-volume *Geology of New Hampshire* (1871), produced many probable first ascents of numerous 4,000-Footers in the White Mountains, either by Hitchcock or by his survey assistants. Likely first ascents were made on the Bonds, the Hancocks, and Zealand Mountain, among others.

Discover Thousands of Local History Books
Featuring Millions of Vintage Images

Arcadia Publishing, the leading local history publisher in the United States, is committed to making history accessible and meaningful through publishing books that celebrate and preserve the heritage of America's people and places.

Find more books like this at
www.arcadiapublishing.com

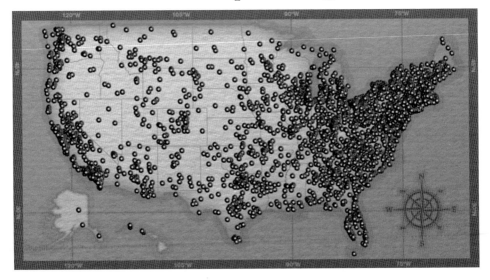

Search for your hometown history, your old stomping grounds, and even your favorite sports team.

Consistent with our mission to preserve history on a local level, this book was printed in South Carolina on American-made paper and manufactured entirely in the United States. Products carrying the accredited Forest Stewardship Council (FSC) label are printed on 100 percent FSC-certified paper.

MADE IN THE USA